Is it magnetic?

Written by Clare Helen Welsh

Illustrated by Nathalie Ortega

Collins

The shark is rubber.

Will the magnet pick it up?

No.

Is the bamboo shoot magnetic?

Will the magnet pick up a book?

No.

Will the magnet pick up coins?
They are metal.

Yes! Look at the chain!

The magnet picks up coins.

Coins are in the air!

They are magnetic!

Is it magnetic?

 After reading

Letters and Sounds: Phase 3

Word count: 52

Focus phonemes: /ai/ /oo/ /*oo*/ /ar/ /oi/ /air/ /er/

Common exception words: the, no, are, they

Curriculum links: Understanding the world

Early learning goals: Reading: children read and understand simple sentences; use phonic knowledge to decode regular words and read them aloud accurately; read some common irregular words

Developing fluency

- Your child may enjoy hearing you read the book.
- Read the left-hand pages while your child reads the right-hand pages. Check they use a different tone for questions, and add emphasis to sentences ending in exclamation marks.

Phonic practice

- Challenge your child to read the /oo/ words. Ask: Which have the /oo/ sound as in "cook" and which have the /*oo*/ sound as in "doom"?

  shoot   book   bamboo   look

- Ask your child to read these multisyllabic words, breaking them into syllables to help them.

  mag/net/ic   bam/boo   rubb/er

Extending vocabulary

- Challenge your child to find the word or words with the opposite meaning to:

  are   in the air   is   Yes!

  Choose from:

  on the ground   No!   are not   is not